P8-ARM-589

GATEKEEPER

GATEKEEPER

poems

PATRICK JOHNSON

MILKWEED EDITIONS

Published 2019 by Milkweed Editions
Printed in Canada
Cover design by Mary Austin Speaker
Cover photo illustration by Adam Ferriss. Source photograph by Jean-Erick Pasquier/
Gamma-Rapho, via Getty Images
19 20 21 22 23 5 4 3 2 1
First Edition

Milkweed Editions, an independent nonprofit publisher, gratefully acknowledges
sustaining support from the Alan B. Slifka Foundation and its president, Riva Ariella
Ritvo-Slifka; the Ballard Spahr Foundation; *Copper Nickel*; the Jerome Foundation;
the McKnight Foundation; the National Endowment for the Arts; the National Poetry
Series; the Target Foundation; and other generous contributions from foundations,
corporations, and individuals. Also, this activity is made possible by the voters of
Minnesota through a Minnesota State Arts Board Operating Support grant, thanks to
a legislative appropriation from the arts and cultural heritage fund. For a full listing of
Milkweed Editions supporters, please visit milkweed.org.

Library of Congress Cataloging-in-Publication Data

Names: Johnson, Patrick, 1989- author.
Title: Gatekeeper : Poems / Patrick Johnson.
Description: First edition. | Minneapolis : Milkweed Editions, 2019. |
    Summary: "What is the deep web? A locked door. A tool for oppression and
    for revolution." Selected by Khaled Mattawa as the winner of the
    2019 Ballard Spahr Prize for Poetry, Gatekeeper is a suspenseful odyssey for
    these troubled times"— Provided by publisher.
Identifiers: LCCN 2019024250 (print) | LCCN 2019024251 (ebook) | ISBN
    9781571315267 (trade paperback) | ISBN 9781571317148 (ebook)
Classification: LCC PS3610.O3714 A6 2019 (print) | LCC PS3610.O3714
    (ebook) | DDC 811/.6—dc23
LC record available at https://lccn.loc.gov/2019024250
LC ebook record available at https://lccn.loc.gov/2019024251

Milkweed Editions is committed to ecological stewardship. We strive to align our book
production practices with this principle, and to reduce the impact of our operations in
the environment. We are a member of the Green Press Initiative, a nonprofit coalition of
publishers, manufacturers, and authors working to protect the world's endangered forests
and conserve natural resources. *Gatekeeper* was printed on acid-free 100% postconsumer-
waste paper by Friesens Corporation.

CONTENTS

. . . on the one hand, living beings (or substances), and on the other, apparatuses in which living beings are incessantly captured.

Giorgio Agamben, "What Is an Apparatus?"

GATEKEEPER

Once I wrote: "There is a point that one can reach when knowing is / too much."

façade (convincing)

> instinct
> the animal has
> knowledge
> the animal has
> a life

Look: the reflection of a light
shining outside the enclosure. On the glass a number of reflections.
On the surface of the glass
fingerprints where visitors like me have approached the animal exhibited.

The panels of glass don't solve the smell issue
of the decay inside.

On the other side of the glass this snake's single
interior perspective—more reflections. Two sections
of infinite positions. Look: either side
of a futile window into a world.

Another perspective then another
(like the foliage-printed façade that covers
the wooden structure hidden from view
inside the herpetarium).

Look: is this façade for the snake or me?
Actual bodies contained therein. I need
to remember. It's easy to be abstract.
They have eyes. They are nocturnal but can see.

Steve gestures to his friend and says he just got out of jail, not revealing why he was in. I impale the lime at the bottom of my drink with a straw. Talking about his terrariums, the ex-con seems benevolent. He tells us how he collects rocks and places them in jars with different plants that he buys on the internet. He says you have to set them near a window, not water them too much, keep an eye on them to prevent mold. I tell him that I want him to make one for me. He says that he will, but I don't think he'll remember. He pulls out his phone and shows me a few pictures. Lit by the sunlight coming through a doorway, the leaves of a fern arrayed across the glass. In a larger jar there are three different plants sharing the same space. For a moment I'm small and live in a chamber.

viewer (exacting)

one long road—

the glare
of headlights
the pupil
increased

A shape becomes a deer but only when—after a knock beneath
the chassis—I see its torso in the rearview.

- It's different in the lab; dissection is bloodless.
  Animals come complete and vacuum-sealed.

- An abdomen is plain anatomy. The liver of the rat
  looks curved like the pistil of an iris.

- Along its two uterine horns lie ten gray sacs:
  inseminated for this—my—moment.

- Say there is a way I could open (under
  a microscope) an idea and see its veins colored blue.
  Its offspring pinned clean and didactic.

Steve interrupts and asks if I've heard about the different levels of the internet. I shake my head. First there are websites with known addresses—the common web. Actually level zero, he says. Then there's the visible web, level one, the part of the internet searchable by most search engines. Not all parts of level one are accessible. Some pages are protected by personal passwords or other limits.

So, there are millions of websites that I can't see because they're underground. This is the first level of the hidden web. Levels two and below require specific software, hardware, passwords, and/or programs to gain access. The look on Steve's face is unrelenting. It's as if someone has applied pressure to my temples. They call it the deep internet, the dark internet, the undernet, the hidden web, the dark web, he says, and I'm aware that my eyes just blinked. Here, a person's activity takes a random route through others' computers without those people knowing. The individual becomes invisible.

law (careful)

A solid transferred to a gaseous state
is called sublimation. This is fitting for a body
wishing to be a mind.

Deposition (the analogous term for a gas) is just
and involves evidence that others don't have.

Back at his apartment Steve shows me how he became an Empath. He moves the mouse on his desk—the music on his computer resumes—and makes room for another beer among the three empties. He opens a program and we watch different messages appear while it loads. He clicks a button. "Use a New Identity." A window opens. "You are now free to browse the Internet anonymously." Empath: someone who can hack through others' computers.

I ask him how he got to this. I don't know, he says, shutting his door, returning to his seat, and looking at me for the first time since we got to his apartment. What he says strikes me with a strange conviction: that there's nothing to stop him is reason enough to keep going.

I'm glad Steve thought to invite me out after our project meeting because I haven't been out much in the last few months. I barely know him, but he has this way about him—where he likes people to know he's a man in charge.

west (american)

>   the doubt
>   a scared child
>   slipping into bed
>   with me

From the parking lot we see it, blue;
first just the blue, like the single stroke of a brush
on a piece of china, and then, through the trees,
on a branch, it takes a shape we all know: bird,
the word iridescent between our teeth.
When we were younger, we never imagined
feeling this way, which is to say we still feel alone,
not knowing how to spend our days, but already
we look into the mirror and think that we are
too young to have to see the skin around our eyes
hang down. When we were younger, we thought
that by this time we would have more to say
when we saw this bird, to speak its plastic beauty,
to know what it's for. Instead we stand, look, and
after a moment approach it. We don't want to scare it
away, but we want to get close. Our desire to see
is unanimous. It stands there, a practical machine
in repose, about to course into action. Steps closer
and we see its wings shellacked, pneumatic.
This is it, we think, seeing something capable of flight
here, seemingly displayed for us. Somewhere
we learned about the speckled eggs of a songbird,
how another species of bird will lay similar eggs
in the first bird's nest, so she is made to think

the hatchling is her own. Maybe this is one of them,
maybe this bird is sitting in a nest. It does not sing,
or call us away, but we see a patch around its beak,
a place where the skin is pocked and bare, black
like the face of the mountain. We see a patch
where feathers have come loose around its eyes.
Now we see the bird's face. It's covered in small mites
that move slow and total, so that we can hardly see,
through the mites, its black eye. The thing stares back,
and its stare could be anyone's.

The Hidden Wiki links to a number of sites, most of which I don't remember. Child porn and black markets, yes, but I'm left with the guilty adrenaline aftermath of more totalizing terror. I tilt my beer can back. The software is enough to keep us from getting caught, I think.

Steve tells me Empaths are assaulted, virtually, when they try to get to levels of the internet with more power.

I ask who has been assaulted. People on forums, he says.

After he hears the sound of a bottle dropped from the curb to the street outside, he pulls on the string of the blinds. To the left then to the right, three times, trying to get the lowest slat to reach the bottom of the sill, until realizing it's as low as it can go.

logic (always)

                              multiplied by a value of 1
                              an equation
                              remains the same
                              $1 = .999$ repeating
                              becomes less
                              and more

This scaled skin. A light
of yellow clouds as we lie awake.
Our wilted eyelids.
To be left with logic
as a kind of curse.
A night of forked tongues.
A night that undressed us
with a tired opiate.
Even a windless dawn.
A powdered-gypsum floor.
We rise through a space in a wall
and wait for water
to return to water.
All we can manage is to slow
our single body.
Still, a distance
between us and us.
Where do we go from here
if not underground?
What more than our being here
traumatic and post-traumatic?
Our mouth drinks dehydration

by an end of an endless spoon.
An unknown surrounding.
The musk of our fear rises
like the swarming
of a single locust
that takes with it whatever.

Warehouse 3 – Current experiment: Cold tolerance test. (Water)

Attempt no.	Water temperature	Body temperature when removed from the water (rectal)	Body temperature at death	Length of time in water	Time to death
3	3.9°	25.7°	24.9°	45'	45'
4	5°	28.2°	28.2°	79'	86'
9	4.2°	26.7°	26.6°	71'	71'
12	4.1°	27.8°	27.5°	94'	101'
14	4.5°	28.7°	25.7°	61'	104'
15	4.5°	27.8°	26.6°	54'	65'
21	4.0°	27.8°	26°	60'	84'

I tell my doctor that it was while making sense of a chart I found on the internet that the panic started. He tells me it's common for young professionals to feel some stress. And that it can come in unpredictable increments.

empath (committed)

> proof that to save it
> condemn it—
> one is healthy and sane
> one is diseased and mad
> one sees the other
> through infected eyes·
> Δ the cure is disease itself

Empath (17:27:35): reading this is just another reminder of how i don't and will never feel like i deserve you.

Anon1 (17:27:42): do you wanna talk

Empath (17:28:51): sure

Empath (17:28:59): as a warning, i feel really emotional right now.

Empath (17:29:09): and you're probably going to ask me about it and it's going to be hard for me to tell you about it.

Anon1 (17:29:31): do you wanna think about it first

Anon1 (17:29:34): and then type it out?

Empath (17:29:41): yeah

Empath (17:29:46): thanks

Empath (17:33:21): idk

Empath (17:35:41): i'm feeling upset by the chart and the rape forums while thinking about how much better of a person you are than me, and how i think i love you, and how i feel like i don't deserve those things when there are people being experimented on in warehouse 3. i mean i knew but i didn't know.

Anon1 (17:36:02): sorry

Empath (17:36:23): don't be sorry.

Anon1 (17:36:51): i haven't shown anyone with a real emotional capacity so i wasn't expecting that

Empath (17:37:01): i wasn't expecting it either.

Empath (17:37:41): when you show me things like this, it's this reminder that there's so much about you that i don't know. and i don't feel the same because i feel like you know everything about me.

Anon1 (17:37:53): that's a part of it though

Anon1 (17:37:59): getting into a person's head as a way of showing how much we don't know beyond the surface.

Anon1 (17:38:03): i'm just saying this is a way of making that apparent

Anon1 (17:38:09): you're doing important things too

It's not long before an anonymous user on a forum agrees to tell me more.

I spend the rest of the night fooling myself into believing I'm working. Really I've turned my attention toward our exchange completely.

I half-lie and say I'm a journalist working on a long-term assignment while my newspaper is in the process of converting to online-only. This feels closer to the truth than admitting what I really want, which is the company of a new kind of knowledge.

No one has ever asked me before if I have a favorite sibling or how often I shave. It's strange, how even though there are things I won't admit, I think I have nothing to hide, and the things that I've become used to hiding—this person seems indifferent to them, which makes me more willing to share. Occasionally I smile, to myself. It's a vulnerable position to be in, seen for the person I am. Or for the one I'm finally becoming—

The light on my bedroom wall has turned red—I'm recognizing white light for what it really is: full of color.

We talk for months without exchanging names.

love (ledger)

                                    a socket
                                    is a space
                                    time seems
                                    like a current
                                    moving alkaline
                                    advancing nowhere

~~A plum: the ease of its sweetness.~~

~~A plum's skin: innocent,~~
~~taut, but unexpectedly tart (the flesh sweeter~~
~~in contrast).~~

~~A plum's flesh: its fibers enfolded~~
~~with the pit, even when overripe, saccharine,~~
~~ugly in excess, a solid thing~~
~~transfigured into liquid when it's touched.~~

~~A plum's mold: a multilayer parasitism~~
~~where one grows insidiously.~~

~~A plum's flies: tunneled and bred,~~
~~having made phases within their host, one thing~~
~~(tyrannical in sum) that falsely appears as a single thing~~

~~or the now second source of flies~~
~~rising from the drain: kept at bay but rash in their habits.~~

An emptying drain, driven by gravity, whose own end
is that all things fall.

I only recall the specifics of the websites later. Here, on my own computer in a café, I reread another account of the deep internet written by Anon.

Turned on inside me is a new faculty or—like an artist rendering with a mirror—maybe now I'm able to see better despite the sight being slant. I take a long sip from my coffee and turn away from my screen. I'm being asked to believe two ideas that seemed before to contradict one another—to see myself as me and as the person I was just moments before. I'm not looking at a magazine but at sediment settling at the bottom of a well of experience, and I'm not sure I have a breath.

I've become an Empath too.

A few things I can't believe. I save some screenshots to my computer. I breathe and feel this is important.

education (self-disciplined)

filtr™
feedr™
a camera lens
futility closes
down itself
eyelid pearl

Anon1 (01:07:13): they leaked the audio

Empath (01:23:09): of what

Anon1 (01:23:11): from the juvenile detention center

Empath (01:23:14): who

Anon1 (01:23:17): the kids

Empath (01:23:20): no who leaked it

Anon1 (01:23:23): they're not even allowed to go in anymore after they got the audio

Empath (01:23:27): who's they?

Anon1 (01:23:36): it's like wikileaks 2.0 but no julian

Empath (01:23:42): where can i hear it

Empath (01:23:44): did chelsea do it

Anon1 (01:23:49): they're trying to get it taken down

Empath (01:23:52): is it real

Anon1 (01:23:59): people are doing it across the country

Empath (01:24:07): doing what

Anon1 (01:24:21): ok here i got a transcript

Empath (01:24:26): can i put this in a story

Anon1 (01:24:29): hacking in and interviewing these kids in jail

Anon1 (01:24:31): "I'm locked inside of like a steel door."

Anon1 (01:24:33): "Some people get in trouble for like other people's actions so that kinda makes you upset."

Anon1 (01:24:36): "I'm way smarter than this, to be in here. I have goals and they can see it."

Anon1 (01:24:44): "Most people see African-American males as criminals that go out and sell drugs, that aren't gonna graduate high school and go to college. And if someone looked at a white person, they would most likely think, they're gonna go to a good college and have a family."

Anon1 (01:24:49): these kids are 9, 12, 14

Empath (01:24:59): can i put this in a story?

Anon1 (01:25:02): "They do sometimes make you feel like you're criminal."

beloved (made-up)

an ambush
in the about face
of your love:
x the future
x the present
x the string tying
together the stems

The axon a way of the brain, the ion
   a way of its making,
                     and the mind a cool variable.
The mind sets out for action. Little dendrites. Axon
                     with the light of myelin, inexact
as reason. Cognition then a function
getting toward a zero, and the one a current
   that inches it along—
         I imagine the freckles on your face,
   not as a swarm of like others
   or a clot, or pigment, or any other mass,
      but as, inside me, the signals fired
across the empty spaces
   to equal what it is I want. How few the materials;
   as the sum of parts, the feeling in the body
         is made and unmade.
                     What is left, then?
   Cholesterols excite through the blood.
The brain sends a signal.

   There's a signal sent.

I start to see things. When Steve asks what I'm working on, I tell him with a laugh that I think the whole thing should be shut down. What about, like, knowledge, he says, democracy. I tell him the internet's bad and there's no going back.

I find it hard to stop.

p u r s u i t (v e s t i b u l a r)

Halfway there
it was night
and I didn't care

By then my skin crawled
like a cat in a bag so I said:
"whatever you are, android or real person—"

but here it did. This guide spoke
like they wanted something
so I sent a face of mine back.

had the profile of a lion
whose beauty never scared me
on screen when it appeared

Then it was day,
the streetlights out.
A second guide

Still I didn't turn from the wheel.
I searched but always found
whatever was unmissable.

I tried to follow the fire of a fox
stalking a mouse out of winter,
with no company in nomads.

or I cared too much—
I looked at the others
to start to see myself.

I've grown more bitter
than a bittersweet stone fruit:
I've seen good and bad.

I ask but my memory has no reply;
the screen was a lesser thing
that I wanted to feel even if

it became a ghost behind me, or
I'd survey it, or at least
figure it out like a lover might.

Standing under the internet
was about taking a flame
into the vision in glass.

There became in me a fear
so diffuse and constant
it felt fostered in my sleep.

Its food chain fed a curious love
of holding a lantern out
to damage after a stormed ship

and then seeing a figurehead
who made me feel
(like no one else

ever made me feel) felt.
In respite from the wreckage
I held a broad leaf over my mind.

I realize the apparatus is just a symbol, the pain and the power still real. The problem with it is I've made myself the controller, and I've made myself the controlled. I've changed somehow, and it's strange how much I can't remember choosing this in the first place. I pull at it, a cord, and it's my body being reeled, toward something I can only describe as my self. Still, it smarts. I'm armed to the teeth against me—in the end I'm not sure it matters who wins. I'm back at it, Empath in my head saying, I'll do what I can, saying, The inhumanity, saying, No control.

Before, there were trees and the fire, which was hardly an object at all.

black mirror (slowly)

broken and entered
three rooms of beauty:
1.   clean and quaint
2.   dark and evocative
3.   causes one to cohere
      and/or come undone

I take a break from my computer. I enter the kitchen
then three other rooms. Beauty out the window
(dust to clean, mine): a quaint vision of children
playing a chalk game. The sky darkens. I take the trash
through the dusk that evokes a filter on a lens.
The moon coheres into fullness—"nighttime."
It's the internet I want to be back at and/or with
another person. This desire, an impulse, undoes me.

It's unclear who has taken over whom, what the purpose is—an experiment in chance operations: who can make the most of pure anonymity. Faintly, the sound of teeth chattering, fingers typing on a keyboard, a person being entered. A random route, hard-wired through the brain, leads to analgesia—an absence of pain without loss of consciousness, the last room of beauty.

war (inside)(beloved)

a grief shared
a grief halved

You particle that lives so wholly apart from the others are the single thing
        that split with a wave of radiation in the last conventional war sure
        you are hypothetical small and indivisible and not specific enough
        for me to make a thought chain of you you expose your purpose
        even as we suppress it the way of this world a dark margin studied
        deep beneath the skin that makes me fail to grasp the words
        to gain the capacity to see an ever-opening now you remain an idea
        of a sequence of changes their careful surveillance taken into custody

Someone starts to laugh. Then it's a group laughing as if someone has told a joke audible only to their circle. As if everyone else is irrelevant. As if their laughter hasn't kept us from our conversation. How we're going to fill our glasses of wine. The rest of us, we're saying, What's so funny? and we don't know—the joke's at our expense. We haven't seen the proof. We haven't heard the joke. We don't know, but these people (the ones laughing) have. I wish that they were all one neck and that my hands were wrapped around it.

I already know their ransom.

wake (systemic)

on my stomach
my head to the left
then back turned
to the right
interregnum of thought
before sleep

Among persons. In place of   a body, thoughts, toward a body. From
a fifth-floor elevator. Regarding a painted apartment, oxalis
growing in an alley, a sedan   "an investment," this. Beneath
a synthetic shroud, which is meant to look   like black leather   on one side
and cleanable.   Against stainless steel surfaces, near ergonomics, through
pneumatic doors, by means of   pulleys and large chains.   Through
hallways traversed by researchers   and nodding endowers with smart
sculptures and windows on a diagonal. Since   after all   a network
is endless   and despite its connectivity   leads to death. Past water,
children with asthma. Into   three or four other elevators. Past philosophy,
what is expected of life.   Despite a sound installation meant
to calm patients awaiting diagnoses, beyond every diagnosis made. Past
gross anatomy   and nicknames. Through hallways neglected
in renovation, collections of dust, a lunch receipt. During a time
for most local hibiscuses. At a site   of colonization and bygone waste.
   Through hallways of a lowest level   closest to
a foundation, past exposed pipes   humid with still air, films diffusely lit
by faraway bulbs. Past   grammar. Around corners
   requiring maneuvers   that make sweat. Down hallways. Beside workstations
in a basement area of chain-link gates manned   by women working
night shifts. Along a fluorescent flicker of vending machines   filled
   with efficient tools. Through hallways, passage of time,   against

linearity. Between buildings that   from ground level seem separate.   In
company of imaginary angels that never   existed. Beyond a notion
    of names for "the body," "the patient," any
    pronoun. . . speech, which belies a fear of death and creates it. Amidst
unfounded biases.   About crime in certain parts of America, spoken
by a white former Marine.   Past needlework.   Behind glass.
Outside of finally   a morgue, which isn't called   "the morgue,"   formally.
    Amidst many surfaces of stainless steel   which must have once looked
clinical but now/tonight/in whichever   post-slavery moment
this is   look covered   with a residue of   having been cleaned
    in a sense.   Beneath a voice that passes on a joke to make
light   replied to necessarily   with a false-sounding laugh. Near a wall
of coronal brain slices—one   smaller specimen   that an employee
mentions to her peers   everything systemic   as being that
of a man   with HIV/AIDS
and talks about   as representing ,   how a brain will shrink
when infected—and a stigma that exists   around most disease among
    healthy people with insurance. Into a chilled chamber   that this ex-
Marine says fills around holiday time. Someone else has said   that she
believes   that when the body dies,   the mind dies with it and that's the end.

In mainstream news articles about the deep internet, journalists explain the process by answering questions that the audience would ask, like "How does a person become anonymous?" "Is my information safe?" and "Can the government find them?"— rather than taking on the epidemic of the interface: rape forums, human experimentation, sex trafficking, terrorist recruiting, and assassination services—but also freedom of speech in censored countries for that matter.

Anon's account is the record of a blank-faced gatekeeper whispering at the border. Now I'm one of the ones putting tape over my webcam, disconnecting my microphone.

they can often be overwhelmed by the sensations coming fr
world around them. Suddenly, the empath feels that he or
"hear" the feelings and maybe even the thoughts of otl

research (uncirculated)

> what a moon
> will do
> to know
> like we want to
> but shine on one side

They've compiled all the data and studied the state of your face:
    after the water (Figure 1);
    when you prove their hypothesis (Figure 2);
    after you have gone without food (Figure 3).

Your hair like an eleventh hour.

For once I can hear death's delegation, coughing, arrive.

If you could tell us, what would you say:
    That the worst was when they diagrammed you starting to fear air?
    Or the video—the liquid in your mouth,
        when the water was a rabid dog, a stretch of fire?

Then you're their image in some corner of the web.

Is this what made me come to envy you?

You're so far from me.

I can't take my eyes off you. I can't take my eyes off you.

I return to the computer and have the feeling of losing grasp of something.

I read that a philosopher thinks there's no immoral way to use technology, but just processes of subjectification and desubjectification. Like waiting in an elevator. The person becomes an object in an apparatus (all technology is an apparatus). When the person leaves, they regain subjecthood, in better touch with who they are, where they are. The question is how long have they been in the elevator.

I check my email and gain next to nothing. I feel as if I'm lying about something I can finally be honest about.

Anon, please—

opening (patent)

> telephone held
> to my ear
> in the hospital bed;
> desire says
> "tell me goodbye"

Seagulls cross the sunset en route from this lot
over the interstate to the next.
A waning on their undersides—blades glinting the air—the image
recalls a fear I've had: to confront an image, a scene, your face—
to slice a poppy's fruit and want to find its petals intact.
How, looking back, it's straightforward.
Simpler explanations, it seems, are, everything else equal, better
than complexer ones.

Often I think of images or remarks that would appeal to Anon's sense of humor. Sometimes I imagine whole conversations we might have.

I alternate between a last-resort mentality in which I contact Anon without restraint and a conservative approach that involves waiting for weeks without a message—and a careful avoidance of putting too much stock in our relationship.

This cycle is fed by moments when Anon initiates conversation, giving me a relief that seems to cleanse me. A conversation that I've played out in my head finally becomes real. A variable clears. Crabgrass, touched by dew, cut days ago, its ends on the whole clean. Up close, they're scarred and desiccated.

When we talk I wonder if Anon will express interest in meeting. The longer that doesn't happen, the more the feeling that initially presented as relief decays into anxiety that I convey around, bared to the wind—We May Never See One Another, I seem to announce to everyone in my midst.

To be preoccupied in this way: I tell myself Anon is just another user and it's fine that we never meet; then again, I think I love Anon as much as I've loved anyone.

More than the sites I've seen on the deep internet, this is the hardest thing to explain to Steve, so I don't.

treason (suspect)

your face
appearing:
as if behind a
1-way mirror
between this
and the next
bright world

I saw what I describe

A level of consciousness beyond what some call real

I was asked in foreign code

Get on board

Dozens of hundreds explain this

I

An infinite amount of information expands inside me

A "multitude" reconfigures the story and starts interpreting it

No one believes my theory of conspiracy

My memory in the process seems written over

I recover what I had before it all unfolded

Different in a way I can't explain

I strain my eyes and swim through the thick light of a setting sun.

I walk through bar after bar—without any intention of sitting down for a drink—from entrance to back exit, tapping people on the shoulder so I can pass by.

Out back I meet eyes with someone leaning against a dumpster with a cigarette in hand, a person wiping their brow with an apron.

I walk the whole night without being noticed.

the name anon (inevitable)

who are you:
abby
ada
adam
ava

Were you a tourist-plagued
monument with its four sides
of Doric order, or a rift
in the earth, converging point
below and ahead, some names
seemingly infinite in number,
individuals amassed into a whole,
or even a body or bodies
catalogued, some living and some dead,
of those who tossed their weight
toward an idea, with
its symbolic-material transfer
into print, until it's impressed
on their minds, staving the rest—

Or were you the single sightseer
who stands, in wonder, before a sheet
of paper, a schematic, its lines
behind gray erasures, a cross section—

How would I begin to prove you?

It seems as if the strung lights in the backyard are here to mock me.

The paper label on the cooler is wet with condensation. Its ink has turned the color of a diagnosis. I stand looking at the cans and bottles floating in ice water. I grab a Dr. Pepper and hold it in my hand, half-submerged. My pregnant cousin is bent over another cooler, adding water bottle after water bottle, sweat accumulating where her dress is caught behind her knees.

I have little to say so I leave the barbecue in the early evening.

The thread is active, sharing places to pirate literature. The last comment Anon made was over a week ago. I find myself messaging individual users, just to see if Anon is hiding from me, commenting under a different username. I talk to them for days before a detail emerges that confirms an otherwise identity. Realizing this, I stop responding to that user.

These exchanges remain in my inbox like leftover food I'm waiting to spoil so I can toss it.

interstices (longed-for)

at least
.think
of me:
dead
here
there

People act as if they no longer know me
I feel as if I'm speaking from inside an error

The realization that without understanding science science could understand me
How I saw myself becoming theoretical to those I once knew

Without destroying me (at least for now) people have found a way to test my
   delicate state
Even with these constant and weak observations they have more to learn about me

This careful superpositioning between multiple worlds revealed in me
I exist between two heretofore exclusive states of life and death

I have no sense of what's at stake for me
The half-life of love et cetera

To disappear in milliseconds: how can I describe this kind of interstitial longing?
I'll never trust whether you use 1) alive or θ) dead to describe me

Gentle measurements will show me at some miraculous state between
Keep the noise low and turn up your signal—keep me uncontaminated

My dad asks if I can knock down a beehive. Halfway up the ladder, I pause to catch my breath. As if I were the only person to consider the moon as it was that day: a fingernail. An individual hand in the sky.

On the radio I heard that scientists have found a way to test the possibility that we could live in a computer simulation.

My dad asks what's wrong. That our descendants have created a program to watch our lives unfold. Our every move as virtual. Their history played out full-flesh.

I climb until I hear the hive. That physicists today can replicate behaviors of the universe at only the atomic level. I watch the bees enter and exit. The order they live by absolute. Is doubt enough to evidence this "real"?

An imprint of an underlying lattice. Measurable.

How long could I wait to knock the hive from the eave? The probability is slim unless the place where we live is already a simulation.

transubstantiation (awol)

                          you meant to
                          send that
                          to someone else
                          i am @ the corner
                          a traffic cone really
                          sorry

I starved myself until it came.

It felt this way—a coming to—as in a city I would come to know.

    As in, Come closer. Or,   But you're coming back,
right?

              An hour passed, and I decided I had to be no-
where.

I left myself in the woods like a body.

Once I went missing, there were myths to be had about where I had
gone,
                                        about why.

Scars can have the order of reminding us,
                    people who reject these theories, that our past is
real.

To convince myself

that the deer feeder meant I was not alone, that you are
human?

that if I waited long enough—

that there would be a shape of light and water, muscle, teeth?

Once there was a kitchen window and beneath it,
held by the branches of a bush,
a cage of bones—I mean a
rib cage.

I catch a glimpse of a Jeep with the license plate "ANON," which strikes me with an irrational yet powerful sense of providence. The thought that Anon would be here on business is a fleeting and near impossible one. Still, for weeks I see Jeeps of every color driven by a hazy silhouette.

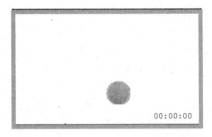

00:00:00

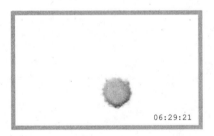

06:29:21

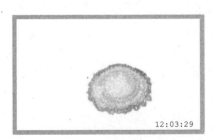

12:03:29

48

White space.

I study cow piss turning orange on canvas. Past the painting there's a screen.

I'm watching time lapse fast: the pill absorbs the drop of water, water dissolves the pill.

The future seems small. There must have been many takes, multiple pills to get this one to split its shape. And then I watch the pill reverse.

Is it a placebo, a drug? Real-life, a trick?

A panic occurs. I'm not sure if I'm the anodyne, the drop of drip, the minutes racing by, the camera, the screen, the gallery, the pain—

war (verifiable)

> the moon will be last
> the last casualty:
> i try to do good
> i forget
> i fall asleep
> i wake up the same
> as before

Like a real war, the screen war hardly seems real.

I think about my side (the one that it seems
I've aligned with). But listen: none of us think much about the war,
our sides on the war, what's at stake.
It's become much more complicated than in the past.

But how to explain the aspect of combat—the small-talk exchange
between martial parties. Is it true to say that everything has changed?

Alignment happens almost by accident. I find myself
among others in a crowd only to discover I'm idling to see something
that isn't there: a basket of fruit, a cache of lost goods for the taking, a lover—
whatever it is that makes us curious.
I've heard whole cities have formed this way.

The smell of spray paint disappears, which indicates that the dream has not only shown me history in reverse but somehow changed it. In this moment I realize I have a level of control.

I am a part of something.

freedom (recourse)

go on touch it
it's hard isn't it?
me if/when i fail
me locked up for life
and me the same me—
what do i think?

○ Run as a client only
○ Relay traffic inside the Tor network (non-exit relay)
○ Relay traffic for the Tor network (exit relay)
◉ Help censored users reach the Tor network   **What's this?**

I comment on a forum:

> The definition of freedom doesn't seem to matter—everyone
> knows what it feels like to become more free. Still, some don't
> know the extent of their lacking freedom, and many willfully
> ignore others' lack of freedom. But real dialogue is like evidence
> of a shared individual search for free will—freedom in the form
> of a conscious resistance to the pressure to just fit in. Most people
> know that assimilating to a norm comes with social advantages.
> But adherence to a norm makes the majority more similar and
> devalues those of the minority in the process.
>
> So do we really choose who we are? Or have I been raised in
> a system and inherited the resources (status, upbringing, and
> "taste") to come to know writing as a solace from a dying world
> where free will is inadequately examined?
>
> Let's say choice is in fact real. If it left me (if, from my minds,
> it was taken), would I know? Would satisfaction in knowing
> a loss occurred come with this change, even as its explanation
> remained beyond my grasp, a flash of light and then a low
> rumble? Would I take the same pleasure as we do in asking,
> Was that thunder?

t r u t h (v e r b a t i m)

> this place
> where i wait
> your message
> ≈ being alone
> ≈ being afraid

Anon1 (22:42:47): it's raining

Anon1 (22:44:12): i'm going to bed now

Empath (22:44:42): ok

Empath (22:47:51): i have this feeling of loneliness that makes total sense to me and i just miss you

Anon1 (22:48:01): what are you doing for food this week?

Empath (22:48:23): not sure

Anon1 (22:48:44): ok. thinking about you a love

Anon1 (22:48:49): *a lot

What my cursor will look like in a decade.

D. says all writing functions "in the radical absence of every empirically determined addressee in general," which is a "break in presence, 'death,' or the possibility of the 'death' of the addressee, inscribed in the structure of the mark."

Sometimes the work seems markless. D.'s theories never work.

When Plato says that the form of the horse wouldn't vanish if all the horses vanished, I no longer see the shadows of the horses' legs, but I start to smell them, bloody, some of them burned, enough of them to choke out the fire—it's hard to breathe with all the blood and hide in the air. The horses, so long until they vanish in reality.

I

Prescription drugs are common on the online market, I've noticed.

Sarcoplex / Anastrozole / Clonidine / Lyrica / Adderall / Valium

Zoloft / Ritalin / Temazepam / Nolvodex / Tetraplex / so-called Phoenix Tears / Aromadex / Femara /

a few of which are cancer drugs:

medicine, philter, remedy, poison, charm, spell, recipe, substance, antisubstance, pharmacia (which means administration of both poison and remedy), and pharmakeus.

D. explains, "The *pharmakon* introduces and harbors death. It makes the corpse presentable, masks it, makes it up, perfumes it with its essence."

I imagine every time a user is caught, there are dozens more at large.

ment, football, Russia, and zoology. The moment they
write, however, the pharmakon of writing poisons the
security of whatever they choose to write about. Writ

s h i e l d (e x p e c t e d)

what happened
the front line
was quick:
1. there   2. there   3. there, there

Look over-shoulder for cities
upon shining metal.
Instead: an artificial-ness lain.
Without a feature, no sign of Nothing,
nowhere to congregate.
An unintelligible million, a million
waiting for a face.

The place discussed;
in dust, enduring a logic.

One could weep. Another wept.

urgent
the message is marked
privacy is the eye
security is the gate
integrity is the gate opening
no matter who's there

Randomness is important. A die can be random, but a computer can only wear the mask of randomness. A computer works blindly and therefore is predictable—unless the machine doesn't follow instructions; then it's considered broken.

A computer uses pseudo-random number generation. True random number generators extract randomness from physical phenomena and introduce it to the program, like an actual die rolled by a computer. The best randomness is found in nature. Movements of the hand. A radioactive source. Atmospheric noise from thunderstorms.

This world can be used to gain access to other rooms, other worlds, previously unimaginable.

A user will be caught by detections of what is only the *pseudo-*random behavior of the network. When the fabric of the interface is made up of pseudo-random transactions between multiple computers, the "random" transactions must have some pattern. This is how Anon could be found.

I have a program that is timed to make the screen replicate evening light when the sun goes down. It's supposed to keep the whites of my eyes white.

war (back-and-forth)

mine eye
mine heart

————————

at war
each delight
in pictures

Consider the white confines of surrender:

Let it be so. Surrender in word. It will be useful.
Weight upon your mind. With this I am, am I? |

I

Mark this mood, the hypothetical end of empire. |

I

Let defeat be defined as a belated victory. |

I

Dislodge the political in order to inhabit the world. |

I

Speak from a place of reversibilities, a drawn-out Oh. |

I

Consider shadowboxes, a masked headless sphinx, a haunting effect, a forensic
mess. |

I

Name a gulf between defeat and possibility and hold it without visible ingress. |

I

See a distance between an image and its husks (deserts, stone lifted from context, indeterminate places within global wheels). |

I

Experience the split screen of the self: a masked figure below an all-reflective surface. |

I

Allow for a problem concerning systems, faux landscapes. |

I

Picture matter as mute witness to survivors. |

I

Speculate what "actually happened." |

I

Unbox that imaginative zone. |

I

I read that authorities have caught a user hired to kill another user. The authorities covered an employee in fake blood and sent a picture. The user was "a little disturbed" when they saw the fake-bloody face but sent the second half of the money. They said they were new to this is all.

fantasy (doggy)

the ant returns
unaware and welcomed
carrying the infection
back to the hill to trojan
its destruction
of self and other

There's a way of looking at a wall
where—even covered by a shadow—the mind
still sees the wall as white. No matter how dark,

lit by a single bulb, constant in my memory,
then less so—my emotion's mouth
turned vacant; then as if I've sheathed it with a cloth,

over its entire face; then wetted, each passage
restricted, unable to breathe, not
knowing what to disclose

when the cloth
is removed

~

Your face remains yours. I'll look at you,
and you'll look back. You'll want to say something,
so you will. The words will cling to their meaning

then fall like husks. We'll have done this
to ourselves. For what little we know
it'll be our last time:

you turning over on your knees, lowering
your shoulders toward the bed, tugging
my thighs behind yours.

I imagine you saying *yeah*
again and again. Even though
we haven't met, this is the ending

I'm ok to suffer—
thrusting with the requisite eros:
between focused and uncaring,

but together
anyway we'll climax.

I'll keep after your body
and almost ignore the distance,
the one you too will have sensed.

It takes an unwieldy confidence to tell Steve and even now, replaying in my head what I said to him in the passenger seat outside the gas station—it's as if my sense of self is sore from the work it's had to do, calling into faculty something that I have online with other users but that's hard to equip in real life—it's confidence ridden with shame, to admit you're something online that you're not among breathing people.

I hear his chuckle that shakes me back to real-world logic: I'm in love with someone I've never seen.

It seems almost impossible—pathological even—to apply this otherwise good feeling to someone on the internet.

Why does it seem that common sense, fitting the norm, apathy, selfishness disguised as confidence—why does it seem like society privileges those over empathy, free thought, and care? It's embarrassing to wash myself of this and deny what I feel. Isn't there a love felt for a parent one has never met?

Anon and I haven't talked in weeks.

One Tuesday, as I'm about to step into the shower, I get a text from Steve asking if I expect anything to happen in real life.

Later, at the Spring Benefit Dinner, I try to laugh when Steve tells three groups of people the same story.

people here (distanced)

                              in the mask:
                              2 hours;
                              holding the mask:
                              5 hours;
                              the mere minute
                              looking at the look
                              of the mask

Even though
you never tell
me

I know that—
because I believe
that people

even in
what they feel

is the worst
part of their life

are more
capable
of good and love

than ambivalence
or spite

or
at least
neglect—

I know that
you care

like I know
that a bullfrog
every night

will call

seemingly
in chorus.

PTSD used to be called nostalgia in the First World War, then irritable heart, then shell shock. Now soldiers ask the driver, Are you seeing what we're seeing? They say, Never tell anyone about this. It's something that happens.

darkness (aroused)

i have left
a trace:
IMG_140305_0024
march4.png
X.jpg

When I sleep, a beam of darkness projects my data
onto the night sky, visible to those who can see
these projections with certain cells in their retina.
I don't completely understand it. Unlike the absence
between stars, this darkness is actively seen,
in the way the black coloring of a caterpillar
can be more remarkable than its green and white stripes.
My entire body and mind: every time I turn,
a new facet of me becomes available to them;
with the curve of my spine, the figures of my dreams,
all of my thoughts—there's a perfect image of me
that I will never see. Most seem to be researchers,
so to them I'm just a case study, but some users are there
to browse. It's scary how much I imagine them
doing next to nothing with me. Often I can only fall
asleep knowing that it might be the time of year
when, after cleaning up dinner and walking to the terrace,
Anon, my one and only, can see me.

When I get home, I look up the drug the doctor suggested I take for anxiety. I can't remember the exact name. It sounded like "rasp." I imagine the edge of a cracked-in-half pill against the ridges of my brain.

It's an antipsychotic. I'm not sure if I want to pick up the prescription. Drugs are expensive. Exposure to trauma by media doesn't qualify as PTSD unless it's for your job.

I sit at the computer for an hour longer than I want to, without doing any research, feeling.

I'll tell Anon my real name.

a single life
never held:
love the thing
away the war
who wants
      it over

NOTES

The epigraph comes from Giorgio Agamben's essay "What Is an Apparatus?" in *What Is an Apparatus?*, translated by David Kishik and Stefan Pedatella.

Page 8 describes using the Onion browser by Tor Project.

Page 14 appropriates and modifies published data accessible via the Onion browser.

"empath (committed)" reworks ideas from Socrates's second speech on madness from the *Phaedrus* (244a–245c).

"education (self-disciplined)" references whistle-blowing acts made by Julian Assange and Chelsea Manning in 2010 with their release of hundreds of classified documents via Wikileaks, which Assange founded in 2006. He is currently incarcerated in Her Majesty's Prison Belmarsh in London. The investigation of rape allegations against him are ongoing. Manning wrote to her supervisor in 2010, reporting that she was suffering from gender dysphoria while serving as a specialist for the United States Army. In a chat log between Manning and ex-hacker Adrian Lamo in 2010, she writes, "The CPU is not made for this motherboard." In 2017, President Obama commuted all but four months of Manning's remaining sentence.

"education (self-disciplined)" also includes a description of and quotations from youth incarcerated in the Dane County Juvenile Detention Center. The quotations come from *Day Room 1* (2017), by Simone and Max, which accompanied an exhibition of photography by Amber Sowards entitled *Captured* (2016), supported by GSAFE.

"pursuit (vestibular)" is a loose translation of the first part of "Canto 1" from Dante's *Inferno*.

"black mirror (slowly)" takes its title from a malapropism of a lyric from "Jungle," performed by Drake and written by Aubrey Drake Graham, Noah James Shebib, Kenza Samir, and Gabriel Garzón-Montano, from *If You're Reading This It's Too Late* (2015).

Page 30 appropriates and modifies a quote by serial killer Carl Panzram, who wrote to protesters demonstrating against his execution while on death row in 1929: "I wish you all had one neck and that I had my hands on it. . . . I believe the only way to reform people is to kill them." Many of his murders only received media attention if they were of light-skinned people. The quote comes via Walton Ford's painting *Condemned* (2007).

Page 34 depicts a moment from Michelle A. Belanger's *The Psychic Energy Codex: Awakening Your Subtle Senses* via Google Books.

"research (uncirculated)" uses language from a song by Burial entitled "Near Dark," from *Untrue* (2007).

Page 36 paraphrases a point made by Giorgio Agamben in "What Is an Apparatus?"

"the name anon (inevitable)" appropriates and modifies language from Maya Lin's proposal for the Vietnam Veterans Memorial.

"interstices (longed-for)" addresses scientific developments related to Schrödinger's thought experiment.

"freedom (recourse)" includes a screenshot while using the Onion browser.

Page 55 references Derrida's "Plato's Pharmacy" from *Dissemination* and *Margins of Philosophy* as well as Plato's *The Republic*. The online market referenced is a now-defunct online marketplace, the Silk Road, once accessible via the dark internet.

Page 56 depicts a moment from Jasper P. Neel's "*Pharmakon* and *Pharmakos*: Drugs, Scapegoats, and Writing" in *Plato, Derrida, and Writing* via Google Books.

"shield (expected)" is an erasure of W. H. Auden's "The Shield of Achilles."

Page 59 draws information from "Introduction to Randomness and Random Numbers" by Dr. Mads Haahr on Random.org. The quote is modified from

Lana Wachowski's acceptance speech for the Human Rights Campaign's Visibility Award in 2012.

"war (back-and-forth)" references Shakespeare's Sonnets 46 and 47. The rest is an erasure of an essay on the artwork of Trisha Donnelly by Michael Jay McClure entitled "If It Need Be Termed Surrender: Trisha Donnelly's Subjunctive Case."

Page 62 recalls details leading to the incarceration of Ross Ulbricht, creator of the Silk Road.

Page 68 paraphrases part of an interview from *The Soldier's Heart*, produced by PBS FRONTLINE.

ACKNOWLEDGMENTS

These poems wouldn't have been realized without the people (all of them: fellow writers, faculty, and students) I met while studying at the creative writing program at Washington University in St. Louis, especially Mary Jo Bang and Carl Phillips. I can't thank enough Amy Quan Barry of the creative writing department at University of Wisconsin-Madison for her mentorship.

Thanks to others who have looked at versions of these poems: Edward McPherson, Sean Bishop, Michael Jay McClure, Matthea Harvey, Martha Collins, Mónica de la Torre, and the late C. D. Wright.

Thank you to everyone at Milkweed Editions for welcoming me into the conversation. Thank you to Daniel, whose encouraging words in 2017 helped make a 2019 publication possible. Thanks to Joey for your sympathetic reading, and to Lee for collaborating throughout the process. Thank you to Yanna—I just like the way you work. Thank you to Jordan, Shannon. . . everyone who has worked, and will in the future work quietly on the project, unaware to me! Thank you to Mary for helping me through our aesthetic saga, and to Rodolfo for putting together my puzzle of text into a book.

Thanks to the Ballard Spahr Foundation and everyone behind the scenes of the Ballard Spahr Prize for Poetry. I'm super thankful to Khaled Mattawa for selecting this book—which is a strange, contradictory, and heavy piece of me—to win the prize after I doubted whether this book was anyone's superlative.

Jack and Alex introduced me to the dark web, so thank you for those experiences, both good and bad. Midwest Story Lab has taken such good care in all components of this project digital and aesthetic, and I appreciate them so much. Thank you to Ali, Amber, and GSAFE for your resistance. I'm convinced that Katie Garth is my secular guardian angel. Simone, Max, Kia, Kendall, Jordan, Crystal, Gabriel, and Travis: thank you for everything you do in my life. Special thanks to Mom, Dad, Brad, Kevin, Becca, and Joe for bringing me back to reality with Sunday night dinners. Thank you to Suzanne, Ken, Clara, and Jacob for checking in on me.

To my eternal accomplice Hannah, the constant emotional support you radiate to literally everyone around you is necessary, and I feel lucky to be so close to your light.

"empath (committed)" is for Hannah.

"education (self-disciplined)" is a wish for the end of incarceration, especially for the children at the Dane County Juvenile Detention Center.

"research (uncirculated)" is for a boy in Matli.

"the people here (distanced)" is for Anon.

PATRICK JOHNSON earned his MFA in poetry at Washington University in St. Louis and completed his undergraduate degree at University of Wisconsin-Madison. He is currently studying to become a physician assistant, and lives in Madison.

The eighth award of
THE BALLARD SPAHR PRIZE FOR POETRY
is presented to
PATRICK JOHNSON
by
MILKWEED EDITIONS
and
THE BALLARD SPAHR FOUNDATION

First established in 2011 as the Lindquist & Vennum Prize for Poetry, the annual Ballard Spahr Prize for Poetry awards $10,000 and publication by Milkweed Editions to a poet residing in Minnesota, Iowa, Michigan, North Dakota, South Dakota, or Wisconsin. Finalists are selected from among all entrants by the editors of Milkweed Editions. The winning collection is selected annually by an independent judge. The 2019 Ballard Spahr Prize for Poetry was judged by Khaled Mattawa.

Milkweed Editions is one of the nation's leading independent publishers, with a mission to identify, nurture, and publish transformative literature, and build an engaged community around it. The Ballard Spahr Foundation was established by the national law firm of Ballard Spahr, LLC, and is a donor-advised fund of The Minneapolis Foundation.

milkweed
editions

Founded as a nonprofit organization in 1980, Milkweed Editions is an independent publisher. Our mission is to identify, nurture and publish transformative literature, and build an engaged community around it.

milkweed.org

Interior design by Mary Austin Speaker
Typeset in Granjon and Didot
by Rodolfo Avelar

Granjon is a serif typeface designed by George W. Jones and Robert
Granjon sometime between 1928 and 1929. The designers based the typeface
on a late sixteenth-century Parisian version of Garamond and named
the typeface Granjon.

Didot was created by Firmin Didot, a member of a prominent French family,
sometime between 1784 and 1811. The Didot family were among the first
to start a printing press in newly independent Greece, where Didot and its
styling are still in regular use. The typeface was inspired by Baskerville's
experimental approach to contrasting stroke thicknesses. It is considered
to be a neoclassical typeface invoking the Age of Enlightenment.